Warm Friends

Senior Authors

Roger C. Farr

Dorothy S. Strickland

Authors

Richard F. Abrahamson ◆ Alma Flor Ada ◆ Barbara Bowen Coulter
Bernice E. Cullinan ◆ Margaret A. Gallego
W. Dorsey Hammond
Nancy Roser ◆ Junko Yokota ◆ Hallie Kay Yopp

Senior Consultant

Asa G. Hilliard III

Consultants

V. Kanani Choy ◆ Lee Bennett Hopkins ◆ Stephen Krashen ◆ Rosalia Salinas

Harcourt Brace & Company

Orlando   Atlanta   Austin   Boston   San Francisco   Chicago   Dallas   New York   Toronto   London

Requests for permission to make copies of any part of the work should be mailed to: Permissions Department, Harcourt Brace & Company, 6277 Sea Harbor Drive, Orlando, Florida 32887-6777.

HARCOURT BRACE and Quill Design is a registered trademark of Harcourt Brace & Company.

Acknowledgments appear in the back of this work.

Printed in the United States of America

ISBN 0-15-306396-3

5 6 7 8 9 10   048   99 98

Dear Reader,

Everywhere you go you can make new friends. There are all kinds of friends—animal friends, people friends, and best friends. Did you ever think you could meet new friends in a book?

In **Warm Friends**, there are a lot of friends waiting to meet you. Turn the pages and learn about yourself through your friends everywhere.

Sincerely,

The Authors

The Authors

Special Friends

4

5

Special Friends

Old friends, new friends—who are your true friends? Wait until you see who the King of the Beasts chooses as his best friend. Think about special friends as you read these stories.

6

Contents

Do Like Kyla
by Angela Johnson

Good things happen all day when two sisters are also friends.

Child Study Children's Book of the Year

SIGNATURES LIBRARY

My Friends
by Taro Gomi

A girl learns from her animal friends to walk, to climb, to read, and to do many other things.

Award-Winning Author

SIGNATURES LIBRARY

Bookshelf

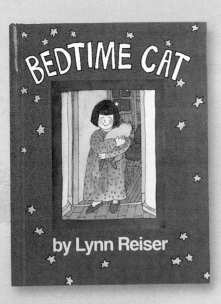

Bedtime Cat
by Lynn Reiser

A girl doesn't think she'll get any sleep until she finds her special cat.

Award-Winning Author

Yo! Yes?
by Chris Raschka

When two boys meet on a street, will they both say yes to being friends?

**ALA Notable Book
Caldecott Honor Book**

ANY KIND OF DOG

by Lynn Reiser

Richard wanted a dog, any kind of dog.

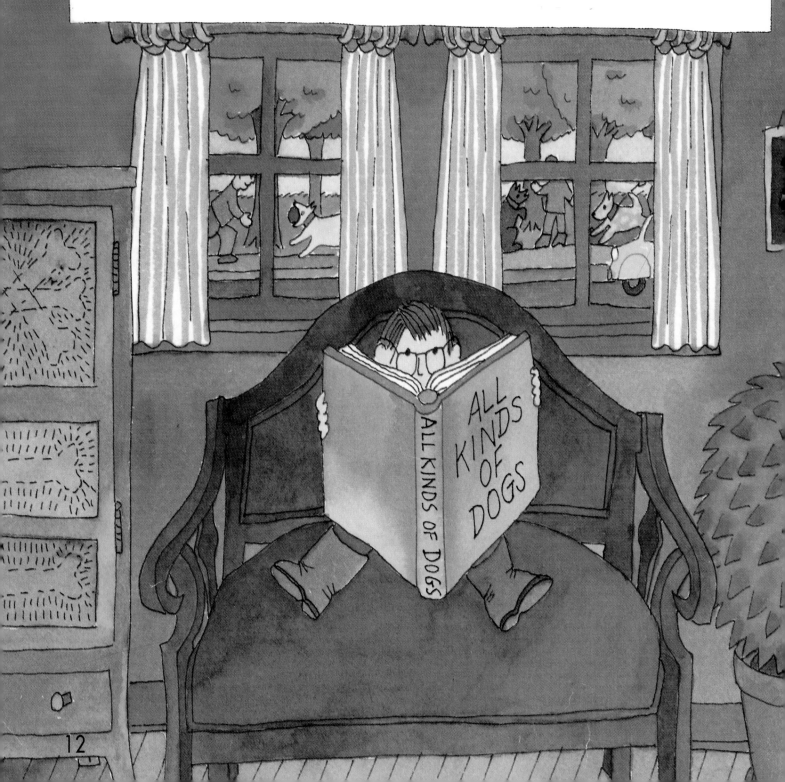

But his mother said
a dog was
too much trouble,

so she gave him a caterpillar.

The caterpillar was very nice.
It looked a little like a dog,

Lhasa Apso

but it was not a dog.
Richard wanted a dog.
His mother said
a dog was too much trouble,

so she gave him a mouse.

The mouse was very nice.
It looked a little like a dog,

Chihuahua

but it was not a dog.
Richard wanted a dog.
His mother said
a dog was too much trouble,

so she gave him a baby alligator.

The baby alligator was very nice.
It looked a little like a dog,

Dachshund

but it was not a dog.
Richard wanted a dog.
His mother said
a dog was too much trouble,

so she gave him a lamb.

The lamb was very nice.
It looked a little like a dog,

but it was not a dog.
Richard wanted a dog.
His mother said
a dog was too much trouble,

so she gave him a pony.

The pony was very nice.
It looked a little like a dog,

Great Dane

but it was not a dog.
Richard wanted a dog.
His mother said
a dog was too much trouble,

so she gave him a lion.

The lion was very nice.
It looked a little like a dog,

Chow Chow

but it was not a dog.
Richard wanted a dog.
His mother said
a dog was too much trouble,

so she gave him a bear.

The bear was very nice.
It looked a little like a dog,

Newfoundland

but it was not a dog.

All of the animals were very nice,

but Richard still wanted a dog.

So his mother gave him a dog.

The dog was very nice.
It looked exactly like a dog.

Just a Dog

The dog was a lot of trouble,

but
it was
worth it.

LYNN REISER

The boy in *Any Kind of Dog* is like lots of boys and girls I know. If they want something, they see it all around them. You see what you wish for.

The story came to me when I was just playing around with drawings. Every time I went over the art, I kept adding dogs and things about dogs. There are dogs everywhere! Look back over the pictures. What funny or hidden things about dogs can you find?

Lynn Reiser

RESPONSE CORNER

A Dog for Richard

Which **dog** do you think is the **best** dog for Richard?
You can make a **dog poster** to show that dog.

You will need:

Dog-shaped or square paper • Markers
Magazines • Scissors • Glue

- **Draw** the dog or cut a picture from a magazine.
- **Write** the dog's name.
- **Tell** why it is the best dog for Richard.

When your poster is finished, you can
- **Share** it with classmates.
- **Vote** for the best dog.

THE LION AND THE MOUSE

An Aesop Tale Retold

by Mary Lewis Wang
illustrated by David Slonim

The little mouse
ran out of his house.
He wanted to have
some fun.

He ran up the lion.

He ran down the lion.

"Stop!" said the lion.
"Your play time is over, mouse.
Now I will eat you."

The mouse said, "Let me go!"
The lion said, "I could say yes. I could say no.
Lions have the say. And I say no."

"Big lion," said the mouse, "a mouse is not good to eat. Let me go, good lion. Then I will help you. I will do something good for you."

"You help a lion?" said the lion.
"A little mouse like you? We lions, you know,
are so-o-o-o big. What could a little mouse do?"

The mouse said, "Just let me go.
Then you will find out, big lion."

The lion did not know about that.
But he liked this little mouse.

The lion said, "I could say yes. I could say no. Lions have the say. And I say . . . go!"
So the little mouse went.

The next time the little mouse ran out of his house, he saw the lion in a net. The lion could not get out. "Help! Help!" said the lion.

The little mouse ran to the lion.
He nibbled at the net.
He nibbled, nibbled, nibbled.

The net came down. The lion came out.

The happy lion said, "What a big help you are!
I do say so."
Said the mouse, "A little mouse is big, too, you know."

Aesop

Aesop was an African storyteller. He lived long ago in a country called Greece. Aesop told fables. Fables are short stories about animals who act like people.

For a long time, no one wrote down Aesop's fables. Parents just told them to their children who later told the stories to *their* children. Now Aesop's fables are known all over the world because they teach wise lessons.

Story with a String

In Africa, some people use a string to tell a story about a mouse. String is wrapped around the fingers on one hand. As a story is told, the string is unwrapped. At the end of the story, the mouse is free just like the lion in the story you just read.

You will need:

construction paper

yarn

scissors

glue

tape

1. Make a paper mouse with a long tail.

2. Hold the mouse in one hand, and wrap the tail around each finger on the other hand.

3. Unwind the yarn as you tell what happens in the story.

Take your mouse home, and share your stories with your family. Ask someone in your family to tell a story, too.

Lions

Lions are wild cousins of house cats.
This is a female lion and her young cubs.
How many cubs do you see?

Most wild cats live alone.

But lions are different.

Lions live in groups called *prides*.

This pride of lions is out hunting for dinner.

This male lion is doing what lions do a lot.
He is taking a nap!

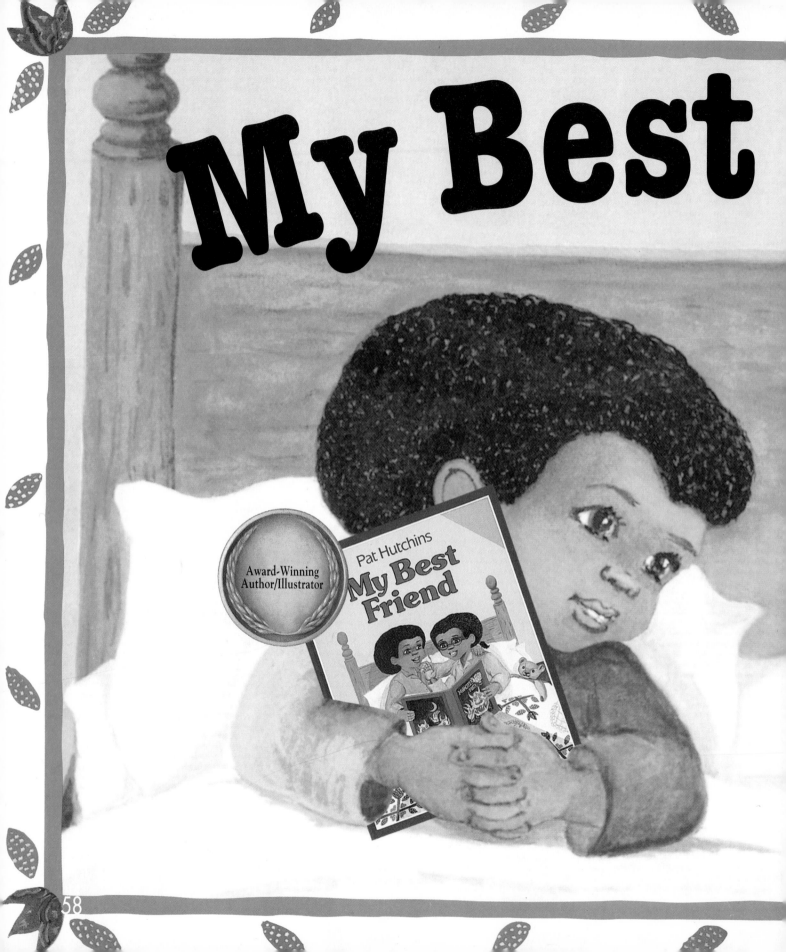

My Best

Award-Winning
Author/Illustrator

Pat Hutchins
My Best
Friend

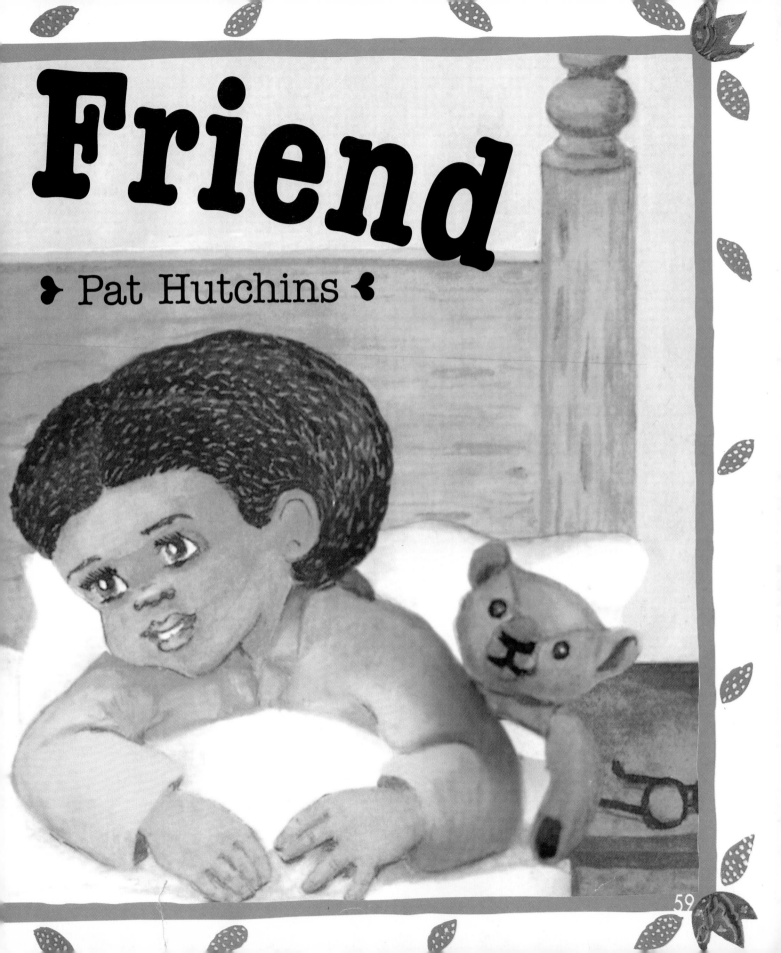

Friend

➤ Pat Hutchins ❤

My best friend is coming
to spend the night.
I'm glad she's my best friend.

My best friend knows how to run faster

and climb higher

and jump farther than anyone.
I'm glad she's my best friend.

My best friend can eat spaghetti with
a fork and doesn't drop any on the table.

My best friend knows how to paint good pictures and doesn't get fingermarks on the paper.

My best friend knows
how to untie her shoelaces

and how to do up the buttons
on her pajamas.

My best friend knows how to read.
I'm glad she's my best friend.

My best friend thinks
there's a monster in the room.
But I know there isn't.

I know it's only the wind
blowing the curtains.

And I know if I close the window,
the curtains won't blow.

"I'm glad you're my best friend,"
said my best friend.

74

❥ Pat Hutchins ❥

Dear Boys and Girls,

I had a best friend who I thought was better than me in almost everything. She beat me at many things—even tennis. But I think I could always draw better. These things didn't matter though, because we were best friends.

Everyone has something that he or she is best at doing. That's why we can help each other. That's why we can be best friends.

Your friend,

Pat Hutchins

Pat Hutchins

My Friend

My friend is nice.
We like to play
We play together every day.
We laugh and cry
and laugh again
Because, you see, we're
   friends,
      friends,
         friends!

by Jane Zion Brauer

"Princess to Duchess"
Brenda Joysmith
Emeryville, California

Response Corner

What a Good Friend!

Best friends can share many things. Make a book about a friend. Then give it to your special friend.

Making a Friendship Book

1. Fold two pieces of paper in half. Staple them together.

2. Make a cover for your book.

MY GOOD Friend

My friend can play.

3. On each page, write one thing your friend can do and draw a picture about it.

After you make your book, you can
- read it to your friend.
- give it to your special friend.

Splash, Splash

by Jeff Sheppard

illustrated by Dennis Panek

A bee fell in the water,
he went buzz, splash, buzz.

When a bee falls in the water,
that's what a bee does.

Bee says:

buzz, splash,

buzz, splash,

buzz.

A mouse fell in the water,
and much to his surprise,

he got water in his ears,
he got water in his eyes.

Mouse says:
squeak, splash,

squeak, splash,

squeak.

85

A pig fell in the water
as he dreamed of eating cake.

He was about to have a bite,
when he landed in the lake.

Pig says: oink, splash,

oink, splash,

oink.

89

A dog fell in the water.
You know what he did then?

He liked it *sooooo* much
that he fell in again!

Dog says:

ruff, splash,

ruff, splash,

ruff.

A cow fell in the water.
She looked a little grim.

Cows like to wade,
but cows don't like to swim.

Cow says:
moo, splash,

moo, splash,

moo.

97

A duck fell in the water,
and ducks understand

paddling in the water
beats waddling on the land.

Duck says:
quack, splash,

quack, splash,

quack.

A cat fell in the water.
She wasn't pleased at all.

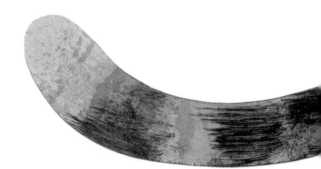

When cats fall in the water,
they look very, very small.

Cat says:

meow, splash,

meow, splash,

meow.

105

A frog fell in the water,

with his flappy, froggy feet.

Splashing in the water
can be oh, so very sweet.

Frog says:
ribbit, splash,

ribbit, splash,

ribbit.

109

Diving and swimming,
wading and playing,

see if you can hear
what the animals are saying.

buzz

Dennis Panek

Working on this book was great. I love pets. I love water. I love colors.

To make my pictures, I used lots of cutout shapes from colored paper. My favorite colors are blue and brown. I like the blue of the ocean and the brown of the trees.

Colors have a lot of meaning. If you paste them down in a certain way, you can tell a story. Stories come from the art you create.

Dennis Panek

RESPONSE CORNER

ANIMAL PICNIC

The animals made a lot of noise falling into the water. Now they are making noise eating lunch. You can make a page for a class book about how animals eat.

The cow is eating corn.
Cow says moo, crunch, moo,
Crunch, moo.

1. **Draw an animal eating lunch.**

2. **Write what the animal is eating.**

3. **Tell what sound it makes.**

4. **Put the pages together to make a class book.**

5. **Read the book together.**

Hop

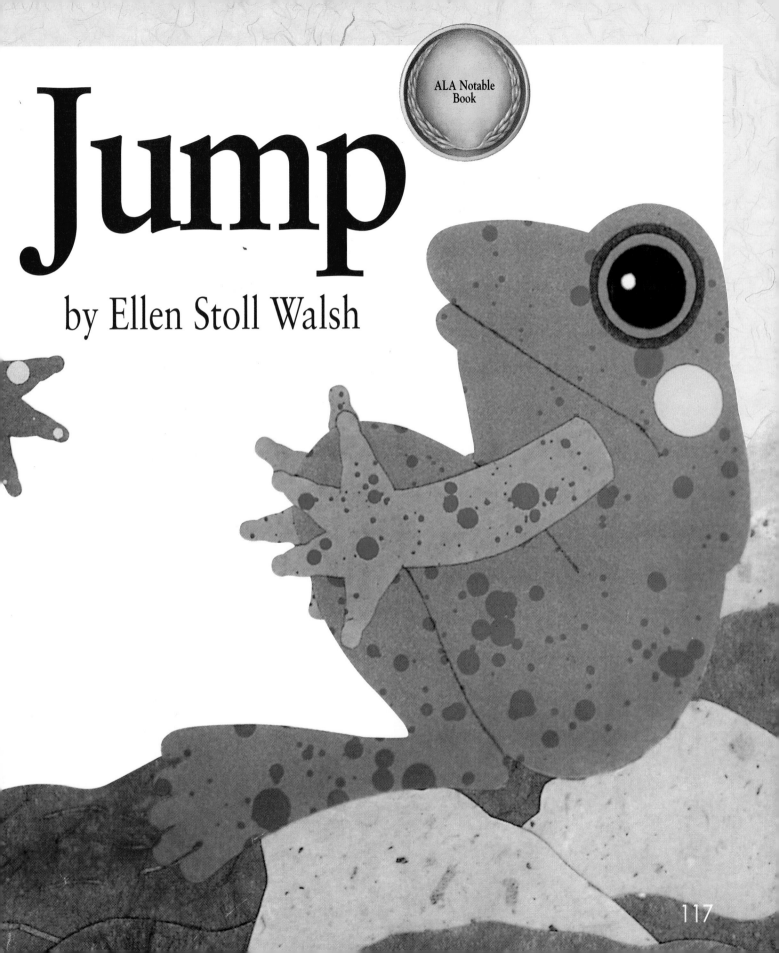

Jump

by Ellen Stoll Walsh

ALA Notable
Book

"Here they come," said Betsy.

119

"And there they go. Hop jump, hop jump. It's always the same," she said.

Betsy watched some leaves float down—
leaping, turning, twisting—always different.

Then Betsy tried. She couldn't float.

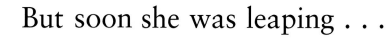

But soon she was leaping . . .

and turning . . .

and twisting.

124

"It's called dancing," she said.

But along came the other frogs, hop jump,
hop jump.

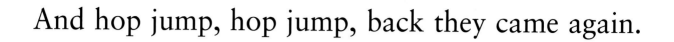

And hop jump, hop jump, back they came again.

"Hey," said Betsy.
"No room for dancing,"
said the frogs.

"Then I'll find my own place," said Betsy.
"For dancing only."

Some frogs got curious.

Others went to see.

Before long their feet began to move.

Soon all the frogs were dancing.

All but one.
"Hey, no room for hopping," said the frogs.

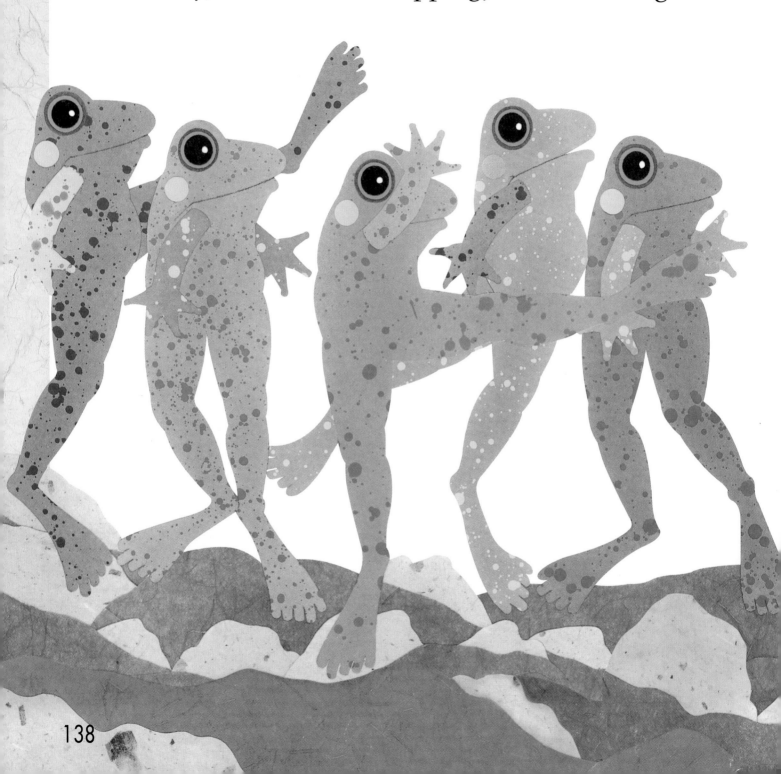

"Oh yes, there's room," said Betsy.
"For dancing and for hopping."

ELLEN STOLL WALSH

What made you write about frogs?

Where I grew up, there were woods and ponds. I liked to play there and watch the frogs. I began to draw and to write about frogs then.

How do you make your pictures?

First, I draw and cut out my frogs very carefully. I cut out the eyes, ears, arms, and often a leg one at a time. Then, I glue my frogs to thick paper.

Ellen Stoll Walsh

I Can

by Mari Evans   illustrated by Mary Thelen

I can be anything
I can do anything
I can think anything
big or tall
OR
high or low
wide or narrow
fast or slow
because I CAN
and **I WANT TO!**

Show Betsy Something New

What if Betsy gets tired of dancing? You can show Betsy how to do something new. Think of what you will show Betsy how to do. Write each step. Ask someone to be Betsy. Show "Betsy" what to do.

Now you can let "Betsy" show you how to do something new, too.

1. Put your finger through the string.
2. Let the yo-yo roll down.
3. Then pull the yo-yo back up.

EEK!
There's a Mouse in the House

WONG HERBERT YEE

EEK!

There's a Mouse in the house.

Send in the Cat
to chase that rat!

Uh-oh!

The Cat knocked over a lamp.

Send in the Dog
to catch that scamp!

Dear me!

The Dog has broken a dish.

And now the Cat is after the fish.

Send in the Hog
to shoo that Dog!

Oh my!

The Hog is eating the cake.

Sending the Hog
was a big mistake.

Send in the Cow.

Send that Cow NOW!

Oh no!

The Cow is dancing
with a mop.

Send in the Sheep
to make her stop!

Goodness!

The Sheep is tangled
in yarn.

Send in the Hen
from the barn!

Mercy!

The Hen is laying eggs
on the table.

Send in the Horse
from the stable!

Heavens!

The Horse kicked a hole
in the wall.

Send in the Elephant
to get rid of them ALL!

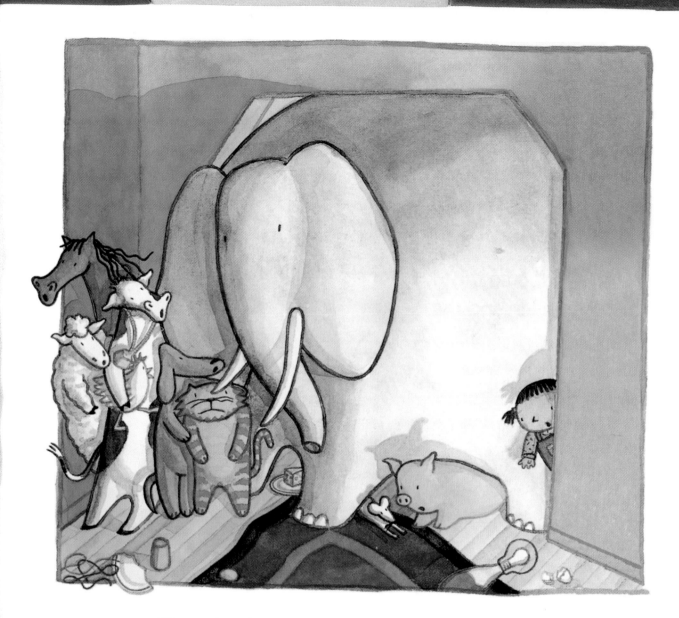

The Elephant was BIG,
but he squeezed through the door.

Once he was in,
there was room for no more.

Out of the house marched
the Cat and the Cow.

Out came the Horse and
the Hen and the Hog.

Out walked the Sheep.

Out ran the Dog.

But then from within,
there came a shout:

EEK! There's a Mouse in the house!

WONG HERBERT YEE

The story for
"EEK! There's a Mouse in the House"
came to me after my daughter was born.
She had a lot of stuffed animals. I wanted
to put the animals in a story for her.
I also wanted a story that makes you turn
the pages to see what happens next.
Did I surprise you?

Wong Herbert Yee

Elephant

by **Langston Hughes**

illustrated by students from the **Harlem School of the Arts**

Elephant,
Elephant,
Big as a
House!

They tell me
That you
Are afraid of a
Mouse.

Mixed-Up Animals

dog|cow

All the animals in the house are running after a mouse.
Now you can mix up those animals.
Use two animals to make a new one!

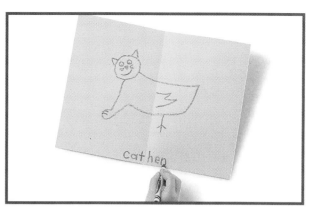

1. On the left side of a folded paper, draw the front half of an animal.

2. Draw the back half of a different animal on the right side.

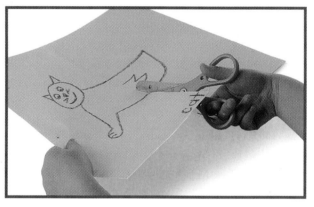

3. Cut your picture in half along the fold.

4. Put all your pictures in a class book.

USE YOUR ANIMAL BOOK TO

- write and tell stories about the mixed-up animals.
- make up names for the mixed-up animals.

Acknowledgments

For permission to reprint copyrighted material, grateful acknowledgment is made to the following sources:

Atheneum Books for Young Readers, an imprint of Simon & Schuster: Splash, Splash by Jeff Sheppard, illustrated by Dennis Panek. Text copyright © 1994 by Jeff Sheppard; illustrations copyright © 1994 by Dennis Panek.

Childrens Press, Inc.: The Lion and The Mouse by Mary Lewis Wang. Text copyright © 1986 by Regensteiner Publishing Enterprises, Inc.

Chronicle Books: Cover illustration from *My Friends* by Taro Gomi. Copyright © 1989 by Taro Gomi; English text copyright © 1990 by Chronicle Books. Originally published in Japan by Ehonkan Publishers, Tokyo.

Mari Evans: "I Can" from *Singing Black* by Mari Evans. Text copyright © 1976 by Mari Evans. Published by Reed Visuals, 1979.

Greenwillow Books, a division of William Morrow & Company, Inc.: My Best Friend by Pat Hutchins. Copyright © 1993 by Pat Hutchins. Cover illustration from *Bedtime Cat* by Lynn Reiser. Copyright © 1991 by Lynn Whisnant Reiser. *Any Kind of Dog* by Lynn Reiser. Copyright © 1992 by Lynn Whisnant Reiser.

Harcourt Brace & Company: Hop Jump by Ellen Stoll Walsh. Copyright © 1993 by Ellen Stoll Walsh.

Houghton Mifflin Company: Eek! There's a Mouse in the House by Wong Herbert Yee. Copyright © 1992 by Wong Herbert Yee.

National Wildlife Federation: "Lions" from *Your Big Backyard* Magazine, August 1995. Text copyright 1980 by the National Wildlife Federation.

Orchard Books, New York: Cover illustration by James E. Ransome from *Do Like Kyla* by Angela Johnson. Illustration copyright © 1990 by James E. Ransome.

Oxford University Press: "My Friend" by Jane Zion Brauer from *Big Bird's Yellow Book Open Sesame Series Teacher's Book.* Text copyright © 1984. Published by Oxford University Press. Untitled poem (Retitled: "Elephant") from *The Sweet and Sour Animal Book* by Langston Hughes, illustrated by students from the Harlem School of the Arts. Text copyright © 1994 by Ramona Bass and Arnold Rampersad, Administrators of the Estate of Langston Hughes; illustrations copyright © 1994 by Oxford University Press, Inc.

Photo Credits

John Johnson,34-35, 114-115; Scala/Art Resource,51; Richard Hutchings, 34-35; Arthus-Bertrand/Peter Arnold,Inc.54-55; Bill Ruth/Bruce Coleman,Inc.,John Chellman/Animals Animals,56-57; Forest McMullen/Harcourt Brace & Company, 141; Richard Hutchings, 144, 166-167; Melissa Mimms 144-145; Santa Fabio/Black Star/Harcourt Brace & Company, 163; Henry Groskinsky, 164-165

Illustration Credits

Lori Lohstoeter, Cover Art; Betsy Everitt, 4-9; Lynn Reiser,10-35; David Slonim, 36-51; Pat Hutchins, 58-75; Brenda Joysmith, 76-77; Ben Mahan, 78-79; Dennis Panek, 80-113,114; Ellen Stoll Walsh, 116-141; Mary Thelen, 142-143; Wong Herbert Yee, 146-163; Renee Braithwaite, Yannick Lowery, Mechelle Hall, 164-165